ROCKS

Library Edition Published 1990

Published by Marshall Cavendish Corporation
147 West Merrick Road
Freeport, Long Island
N.Y. 11520

Printed in Italy by Imago Publishing Ltd

© Marshall Cavendish Limited 1990
© Cherrytree Press Ltd 1989

Designed and produced by AS Publishing

Library of Congress Cataloging-in-Publication Data

Mariner, Tom
    Rock / by Tom Mariner,
        p. cm. – (Earth in action)
        "A Cherrytree book."
    Includes index
    Summary: Discusses our planet's rocks, what they are made of, how they change, the differant kinds, and their uses.
        ISBN 1-85435-194-X
        1. Rocks – Juvenile literature. [1. Rocks.]
    I. Atkinson, Mike, ill. II. Title. III. Series: Earth in action
    (New York, N.Y.)
    QE432,2,M28 1989   89-17321
    552-dc20   CIP
                                                                       AC

· EARTH · IN · ACTION ·
ROCKS

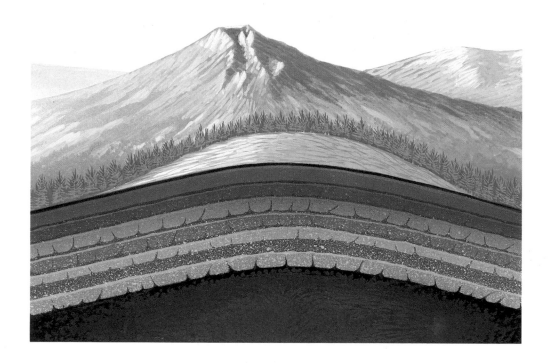

Tom Mariner
Illustrated by Mike Atkinson

MARSHALL CAVENDISH
NEW YORK · LONDON · TORONTO · SYDNEY

Our Rocky World

Our earth is a rocky planet. Most rocks are hidden from view under a layer of plants or beneath cities and towns. Other rocks lie under lakes, ice sheets and seas. But we can see rocks every time we dig our gardens, because soil consists of worn grains of rock mixed with rotted plant matter.

The study of rocks is called *geology*. Through their work, geologists have traced the history of the earth. They also know how to find valuable fuels and minerals in rocks.

You can see bare rock in cliff faces or in canyons worn out by rivers. Many rocks form in flat layers. If the rocks have not been disturbed, the older rocks are at the bottom and the younger ones at the top.

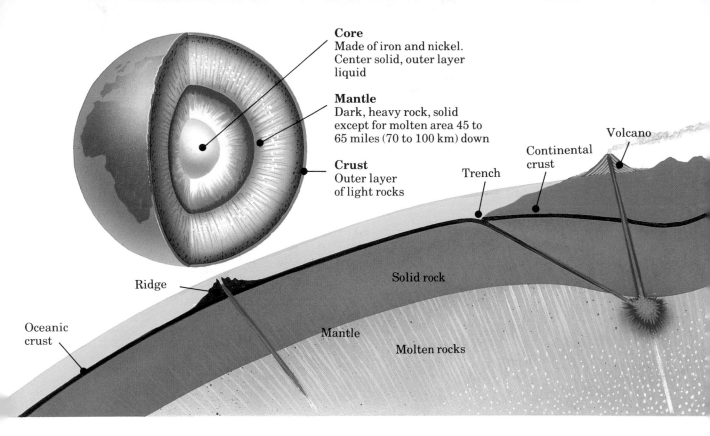

Core
Made of iron and nickel. Center solid, outer layer liquid

Mantle
Dark, heavy rock, solid except for molten area 45 to 65 miles (70 to 100 km) down

Crust
Outer layer of light rocks

Volcano

Continental crust

Trench

Ridge

Solid rock

Oceanic crust

Mantle

Molten rocks

The rocks of the earth's outer layer average 4 miles (6 km) thick under the oceans and up to 45 miles (70 km) thick under high mountains. Between the crust and the core is the mantle, which is made of dark, hard rock some 1,800 miles (2,900 km) thick. The crust and the hard top part of the mantle float on an area of hot, molten rock, constantly shifting.

The earth measures nearly 4,000 miles (6400 km) from the surface to the center. Inside the earth are several layers. At the center is the *core*, the heaviest and hottest part of the earth. The inner core is solid, but the outer core is liquid.

Around the core is another layer, called the *mantle*. It is made of heavy rocks, though they are not nearly as heavy as the substances in the core. Parts of the upper mantle are hot and melted. This melted rock, called *magma*, moves around like a stiff, thick liquid. The top of the mantle and the thin *crust* that forms the outer shell of the earth both consist of rigid, solid rocks.

The Elements of Rocks

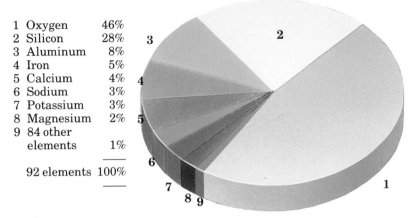

1	Oxygen	46%
2	Silicon	28%
3	Aluminum	8%
4	Iron	5%
5	Calcium	4%
6	Sodium	3%
7	Potassium	3%
8	Magnesium	2%
9	84 other elements	1%
	92 elements	100%

The chart shows the chief elements in the earth's crust. Oxygen and silicon make up nearly three quarters of the weight.

Rocks are made of *minerals*, and minerals are made of *elements*. Elements are pure chemical substances. The earth's crust contains 92 elements, but only eight are common. They make up nearly 99 percent of the crust. Oxygen, silicon, aluminum and iron are elements.

Some minerals, such as gold, copper and sulfur, are also pure elements, but most minerals are combinations of two or more elements. They are always composed of the same elements, combined in the same amounts. Geologists identify minerals from several features, including their color, hardness, specific gravity (their weight compared with an equal volume of water), crystal shape, transparency and so on.

Rocks are made of minerals, but the minerals are not always present in the same amounts. Separate pieces of the same kind of rock may be obviously different. For example, granite paving stones may be white, gray, pink, red or black, depending on the mixture of minerals the rock contains.

The surface color of a mineral may not be its true color. Test by scraping the surface with a penknife or scraping the rock across the back of a white tile. If you try this with the black mineral hematite, it will leave a red mark.

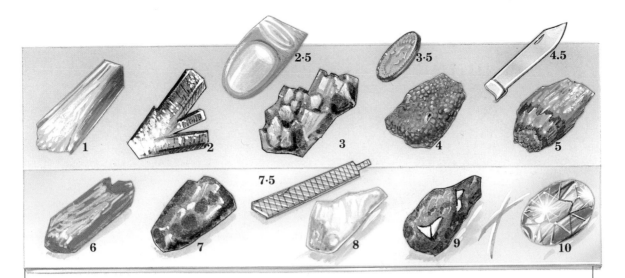

MOHS' SCALE
Each mineral has a certain hardness. Ten minerals are used to make up a table of hardness (named for a geologist named Mohs) by which the hardness of other minerals can be measured.

The softest is talc (1), the hardest diamond (10). Other minerals or common objects can be used to test for hardness. For example, calcite (3) scratches gypsum (2), but will not scratch fluorite (4). A fingernail has a hardness of 2.5. It will scratch gypsum, but not calcite. A steel file will scratch quartz (7), but not topaz (8). Softer minerals (1-5) can be scratched by glass; harder ones (6-10) will scratch glass.

Crystals form when molten rock cools and becomes solid. It sets in certain shapes. Geologists can tell which particular mineral formed the crystals from the shape. Crystals are often very beautiful, and some, such as emeralds, are highly prized.

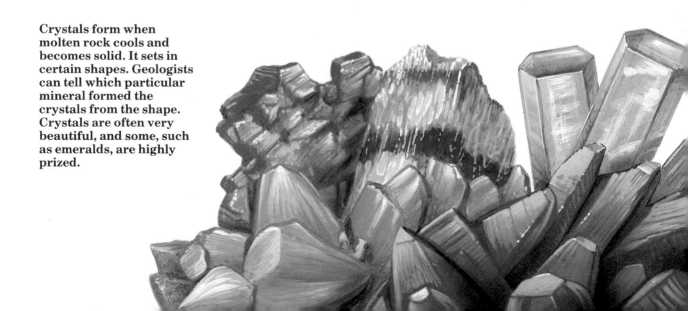

The Composition of Rocks

Granite (far left) is made mostly of two important rock-forming minerals, feldspar (white or pink) and quartz (gray or white). It often also contains small amounts of other minerals, such as mica (black).

Rock crystal (left) is a colorless, almost pure kind of quartz.

Limestone (below) is mostly the colorless mineral calcite. Some types of limestone are formed almost entirely from the shells of long-dead sea creatures.

Rocks are made from fragments of minerals pressed and cemented together. There are about 3,000 minerals altogether, but fewer than a hundred make up the most common rocks. The most important rock-making minerals are *silicates*. They are a large family of minerals which are made of oxygen and silicon mixed with other elements. They are found in many kinds of rock.

The second most common rock-forming minerals are *calcites*. They make up most of the rock limestone which is found all over the world. Calcites dissolve in water, and there are vast quantities of them in the sea and rivers. They collect around grains of other minerals and bind them together to form rock. They act like cement in concrete. They also form stalactites and stalagmites in limestone caves.

8

Metals from Rocks

Many minerals are *metals*. Some metals, such as gold and silver, are sometimes found as pure elements in the rocks. But most metals are found combined with other elements or minerals in rocks which have to be processed to give pure metal. Rocks which contain metals that can be extracted are called mineral ores. Hematite is an important ore from which we obtain iron. Much of our copper comes from a mineral called chalcopyrite.

Mineral ores do not look like the metals that are made from them. They are not strong, hard and shiny like most metals. Some are concentrated in layers of rock called veins. Sometimes they have been washed out of the solid rock and are found on the surface as grains of ore mixed with sand or gravel.

An iron ore mine. Iron is extracted from several mineral ores, including hematite and magnetite.

Gold is so rare and precious that mines over 1¾ miles (3 km) deep have been dug to find it. Tons of ore would be needed to produce these gold ingots.

The Changing Rocks

Rocks are always changing. In one place, new rocks are forming; in another, rocks are being destroyed and more new rocks being formed from their remains. Most of these changes occur too slowly for us to notice, but some are easy to see. When a volcano erupts, for example, molten rock called *lava* may pour from the crater. As it cools, the lava hardens into new rock.

Sediments in the Sea

Other changes take place more gradually. After a storm, the water in a river looks muddy. The color comes from *sediment* – mud and sand – which is the remains of solid rock that has been destroyed by the weather. Year after year, millions of tons of sediment that was once rock are deposited in the sea. New sediment weighs down on the sediment beneath it. Dissolved rock in the sea cements the loose sediment together, and eventually it becomes solid rock.

Earth Movements

Newly-formed rock may be heaved upward by movements in the earth's crust to form new mountains. Rocks high on Mount Everest contain fossils of sea creatures, which means that the world's highest mountains must have been formed on the seabed.

Other earth movements force crustal rocks downward into the mantle, where they are melted by great heat to form magma. They may reappear as lava when a volcano erupts, or it may cool and harden into rock underground. These continuous changes are called the *rock cycle*.

THE ROCK CYCLE
Natural processes are always changing the rocks in the earth's crust. When a volcano erupts, magma (molten material) is forced to the surface as lava, and new igneous rock is formed (1). But even as new mountains are created, the weather and other natural forces wear them down (2).

Fragments of worn rock are carried away by glaciers and rivers to the sea (3). On the way, they are ground down into sand, silt and mud. These sediments are spread over the ocean floor (4).

They pile up in layers which are compressed and cemented together to form new sedimentary rocks (5). As these new rocks are buried, great pressure and heat deep down change some of them into metamorphic rocks (6).

Some rocks are forced down so far that they melt to become magma (7). Some magma rises up and cools in the earth's crust. Some appears on the surface as lava (1), so completing the rock cycle.

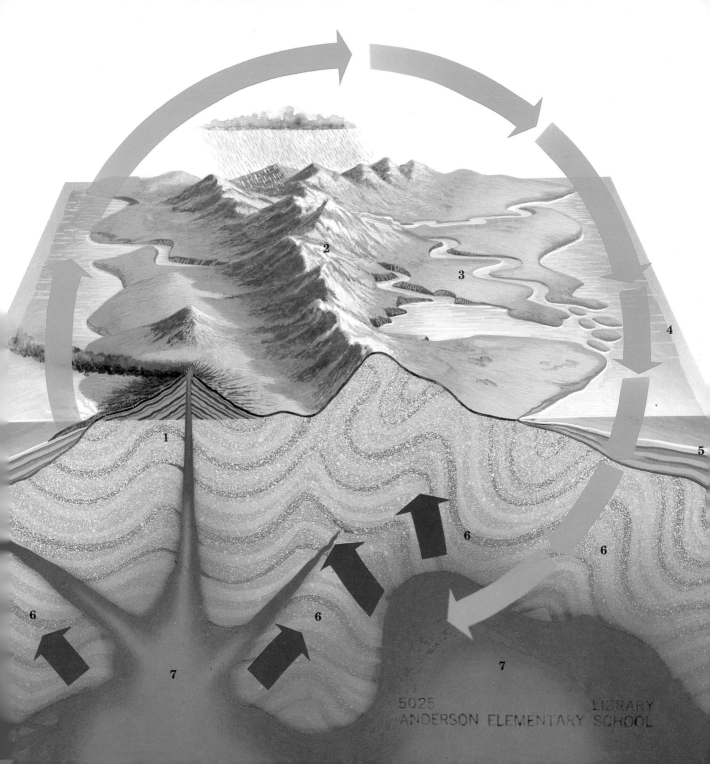

2

3

4

5

1

6

6

6

6

7

7

Volcanic ash

Magma spurts from a volcano in the form of ash and lava. They harden quickly to make extrusive igneous rocks. Magma in underground areas called batholiths cools more slowly because the rocks around them keep the heat in. It hardens to become intrusive igneous rock. Some magma is forced into cracks and hardens into sheets, called *sills* or *dikes*.

Lava flow

Side vent

Alternate layers of lava and ash

Dike

Sill

Magma

Batholith

Kinds of Rocks

The earth's crust contains three main kinds of rock: *igneous*, *sedimentary* and *metamorphic*. Igneous rocks form when molten magma solidifies. Geologists divide them into two main types: *intrusive* and *extrusive*.

Intrusive Igneous Rocks

Beneath the hard outer layers of the earth is a layer of magma. Some magma rises through the overlying rocks into the crust. Some of it accumulates in huge areas called *batholiths*. Here it cools and hardens slowly to form coarse-grained rocks containing size-able mineral crystals. Batholiths often push up the overlying rocks to form *domes*. When the rocks above are worn away, the rocks in the batholith appear on the surface. These rocks are called intrusive igneous rocks. Granite is the most common intrusive igneous rock.

Extrusive Igneous Rocks

Other igneous rocks form from magma that reaches the earth's surface. They are called extrusive igneous rocks. Some form when magma spills out as lava through volcanoes or cracks in the ground. The lava cools and hardens quickly in the air. Because there is not enough time for crystals to form, the rocks are fine-grained or glassy. Basalt, the most common extrusive igneous rock, and obsidian, which is a glassy rock, are both formed in this way. Other rocks are formed when volcanic ash explodes into the air. Piles of volcanic ash form a rock called tuff, while tiny fragments of volcanic glass form a rock called ignimbrite.

Although granite (top) and obsidian are made of the same minerals, they are not the same. They are different because they have cooled at different rates. Granite is formed when magma cools slowly underground, giving time for crystals to grow. Obsidian forms when the magma cools too quickly for crystals to grow. It is a smooth, glassy rock.

Sedimentary Rocks

Sedimentary rocks make up only a small part of the earth's crust. But they stretch like a thin skin over about three quarters of the earth's land surfaces.

Most sedimentary rocks consist of particles worn away from rocks on land and carried into the sea by rivers. The smaller particles are washed into the sea as mud and become compressed into a smooth, dark rock called shale. Sand grains, which are larger, form sandstone. Some sedimentary rocks look like pebbles cemented together. They are called conglomerates.

Water evaporates from the sea, and the moisture is swept into the air to form clouds. The clouds bring rain and snow to land areas, but the moisture finally returns to the sea through rivers. This continuous process, called the water cycle, plays an important part in the formation of sedimentary rocks. Rain helps to break up rocks, and rivers carry worn material, ranging in size from pebbles to sand and fine clay, into the sea. Winds also play their part in the water cycle by blowing loose sand and dust across the land.

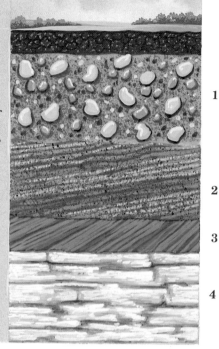

ROCK STRATA
If you could drill down into the ground, you would probably find that the rocks beneath your feet are divided into layers, or strata. Under the soil, you might find a layer of conglomerate (1) formed on an ancient beach. Below it, the layer of sandstone (2) was formed when the sea level was higher, because sandstones are formed in offshore waters. Lower still is a layer of shale (3) formed from silt in deeper water. This shows that the sea level had again changed. Under the shale is limestone (4), formed on a deep seabed. Drilling downward is like a journey back in time.

1

2

3

4

Some sedimentary rocks are formed from chemicals dissolved in water. A rock called oolitic limestone consists of tiny grains of sand, each coated with layers of the mineral calcite and cemented together. Oolitic means egg-stone; the grains in the rock look like fish eggs. Another type of chemical sedimentary rock is made from minerals left behind when ancient seas or lakes dried up. Rock salt and gypsum are formed in this way. A third kind of sedimentary rock is made of the remains of living things. Coal consists of layer upon layer of dead plants pressed into rock. Chalk is a kind of limestone formed from the shells of billions of tiny sea creatures.

Metamorphic Rocks

Metamorphic rocks are rocks that have been changed. They were originally igneous or sedimentary rocks, but great heat and pressure have changed them out of all recognition, just as a lump of dough is changed in a hot oven into a loaf of bread.

Much of the heat that causes rocks to change comes from molten magma that is squeezed upward through the crust. The surrounding rocks are "cooked" and changed. This process is called *contact*, or *thermal*, metamorphism. Around large bodies of magma, the rocks may be cooked for a distance of one to two miles (two to three km).

Rocks can also be changed by pressure, when for instance, they are squeezed together by earth move-

Metamorphic rocks are formed by heat and pressure, which may be caused when magma rises through the earth's crust. This changes limestone into marble. Pressure and heat are also generated when rocks are folded to form new mountain ranges. Shale is changed into the hard rock slate as a result of pressure.

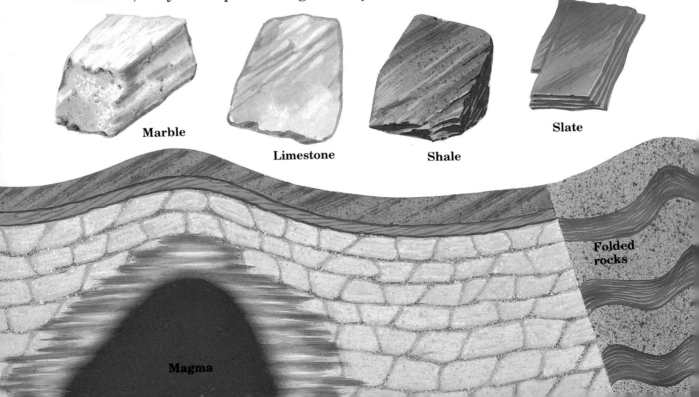

Marble

Limestone

Shale

Slate

Folded rocks

Magma

Marble is easy to cut, polish and make into ornaments, such as marble eggs (above). When rocks are metamorphosed, the molecules in the minerals may be rearranged in layers (below). As a result, some metamorphic rocks, such as slate, split easily into thin sheets.

ments. This is called *dynamic* metamorphism. Often, especially during mountain building periods, heat and pressure combine to cause *regional* metamorphism. The effect of regional metamorphism may be felt for hundreds of miles.

Marble is formed when limestone or dolomite (a similar rock) are changed by contact or regional metamorphism. Marble may be snow-white or colored by streaks of impurities. Slate is an example of a rock produced as a result of pressure. Other metamorphic rocks include hornfels, schist, quartzite and gneiss.

Sometimes minerals in metamorphic rocks are re-crystallized to form new minerals. Garnets, used in jewelry, are crystals often found in schists and gneisses created during metamorphism.

MOON ROCKS AND METEORITES

The earth and the moon were both formed about 4,600 million years ago. More ancient rocks are found on the moon than on earth because there is no erosion on the moon. Missions to the moon have brought back 850 pounds (385 kg) of soil and rock. The moon's oldest rocks are in the mountains, which are the pale areas we can see from the earth. The dark patches were once believed to be oceans. In fact, they are hollows filled with basalt rock that was formed like basalt on earth.

The earth is continually bombarded by rocks, or meteors, from space. They are bits of old planets which are drifting through space. Nearly all of them burn up in the earth's atmosphere and we see them as shooting stars. But some hit the earth's surface. There are two main kinds: rocky or iron meteorites. Iron meteorites are pieces from the original core of a planet, rocky ones from the mantle or crust.

Moon rock

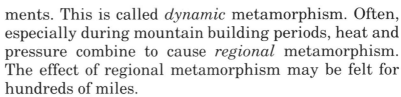

Rocks and Their Uses

Ancient peoples used rocks for many things. They used flint and obsidian to make axes and spear points. They ground grain into flour between stones. They learned how to find metals such as copper and tin, and how to make bronze tools from them. Later on, they learned how to work iron, a harder metal than bronze. From early times, too, they were attracted by beautiful minerals, including gold and precious stones, which they made into jewelry.

Today we are surrounded by products made from rocks. For example, knives, forks and spoons are made from metals taken from metal ores in the rocks. Plates, cups and saucers are made from clay mixed with other minerals and heated to high temperatures. The finest china is made from kaolin, a clay formed when some kinds of granite decompose.

Rocks are used to make building materials. Cement is a gray powder made from limestone mixed with some clay. Combined with sand and water, it makes mortar, which binds bricks and stone together. Add small stones, and the mortar becomes concrete, the most common building material used today. Sand and clay are mixed to make bricks and tiles.

Today we use rocks more than ever before. Nearly all metals come from ores dug out of the earth's crust. Fuels, such as coal, are found in layers in rocks, as are natural gas and oil. These substances are all formed from the remains of once-living organisms buried under layers of rock. By using coal, gas and oil, people have created new industries, including the production of chemicals and plastics. Nuclear power is made by using uranium, a metal ore found in rocks.

Several rocks are used for building. Limestone has been a popular building stone from early times, while marble has often been used for special buildings, such as temples. Granite and sandstone are two other tough building stones, and sand is used to make glass windowpanes. But good building stone is expensive, and modern houses are often built from artificial "stones", made like bricks in factories.

The Opera House in Sydney, Australia, is a modern wonder of the world, made of materials that come from rock. It rests on a platform covering nearly five acres (two hectares) made of 127,000 tons of concrete and 6,000 tons of reinforced steel. The roofs, shaped like shells, are covered with tiles which have a shiny surface like fine china.

Mining

To obtain metals, mineral ores have to be treated in some way. Many are *smelted*, or melted, in order to remove impurities. Another process, *leaching*, involves dissolving the metal from the ore, and then recovering the metal from the liquid.

Aluminum comes from ores called bauxite. The bauxite is *refined* to produce a compound, called alumina. The alumina is smelted to remove the oxygen in the alumina and produce the metal. Pure aluminum is soft. To make it hard, it is mixed with small amounts of other metals. Mixtures of metals are called *alloys*. Iron ore goes through similar processes. Iron is recovered from ores in blast furnaces, and the iron is used to make steel alloys.

Aluminum is obtained from an ore called bauxite, which is usually mined on the surface. Aluminum is mixed with other metals to make light, strong alloys. It can be made into wire, thin sheets for making airplanes and cooking pans or even thinner sheets of foil.

Coal is a rock made from ancient dead plants that have been submerged by water and compressed over millions of years. The more it has been compressed, the harder it becomes and the hotter it burns. Peat is soft, moist and burns slowly. Lignite gives out moderate heat. Shiny, black bituminous, or steam, coal burns with a hot, smoky flame. Anthracite, the hardest coal, burns the hottest.

Peat

Lignite

Steam coal

Anthracite

Making Coal

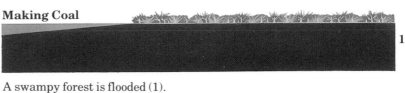

1

A swampy forest is flooded (1).
The trees die, and mud and sand are deposited on them (2).

2

Under the weight, the trees turn to peat (3).

3

The sea level falls, and the forest grows again on top of the hardened mud and sand. The peat hardens into coal (4).

4

Fuel from the Earth

Coal is made up of the remains of plants that once grew in swampy forests. The remains of the plants were buried in the muddy water. The sea level then rose, or movements in the crust made the land sink. Layers of sedimentary rocks formed on top of the buried plants. At first, the material was like peat, with water making up 90 percent of its weight. But gradually the water was squeezed out until it became a hard rock, called anthracite.

Natural gas sometimes escapes from deeply buried coal layers and seeps into the rock layers above. Natural gas is also found in oil deposits. Oil is formed from the remains of tiny plants and animals that lived in ancient seas.

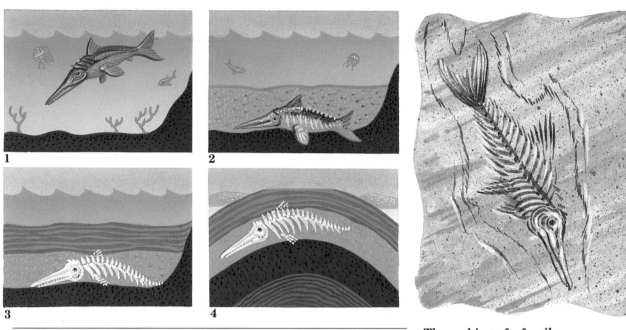

Fossils

Fossils are the remains or traces of animals and plants that lived long ago and have been preserved in rocks. A fossil may be a shell, a bone, a tooth or a complete skeleton. It may be a footprint or a faint impression of a leaf on the surface of a stone.

When an animal dies, its body rots or is eaten. The soft parts decay first, then the bones or shell. Sometimes, however, the body is preserved, and a fossil forms. Fossils form in a variety of ways. A skeleton on the seabed will be quickly covered with sediment. During the course of thousands of years, the sediment will harden into rock. At the same time the skeleton may be *petrified* – turned to stone. The original material will dissolve away, but minerals in the water

The making of a fossil: millions of years ago, a fish died (1) and sank to the seabed. The soft parts of its body decayed, and sediments covered its bones (2). The bones dissolved, and minerals from the water replaced them. The sediments, compressed by more layers above, hardened into rock (3). Years later, earth movements lifted the rocks – and the fossil – out of the sea (4). The fossil itself was found on dry land when the rock was worn away to expose it.

passing through tiny holes or pores in the bone will gradually replace it all. The resulting stone skeleton may be harder than the surrounding rock.

Sometimes minerals do not replace the body of the animal. Instead a hollow, or *mold*, remains in the rock, and you can see the exact shape of the animal, especially if it had a shell. Sometimes a mold is filled with minerals, and a fossil *cast* is formed, which is the same shape, but solid.

Fewer fossils are made on land because there is less chance of an animal's body being buried quickly, though many specimens of creatures that have fallen into swamps or tar pits or buried by sandstorms have been found. Whole "forests" of petrified trees have been found. The molecules of their decaying wooden trunks have been replaced entirely by minerals.

This coelurosaur left its footprints in the mud. The mud dried and hardened. Sediments buried the footprint and hardened into rock. The footprint is a *trace fossil*. Fossilized footprints can tell us a lot about an animal: how heavy it was, how long its stride was, whether it was a meat-eater or a plant-eater, and much more.

Record of the Rocks

Ever since the earth was formed, about 4,600 million years ago, natural forces have been at work on its surface. At first, the surface was mainly molten, but after millions of years, the surface cooled and hardened. New rock was created, broken up and remelted in an endless cycle. The oldest known rocks are 3,800 million years old.

To a geologist, the layers, or strata, of sedimentary rocks are like the pages of a history book. But because of earth movements, erosion and weathering, the book is difficult to read. The pages are often torn, turned upside-down, scattered over a wide area or, in many places, simply missing.

Fossil Clues

Fossils that geologists find in the layers help them date the rocks. If they find the fossil of an animal that lived 200 million years ago in a rock layer, they know that the rock is about 200 million years old. The rocks above may contain older or younger fossils. If they are older, the geologist will know that an upheaval has taken place.

Geologists divide the history of the earth into periods according to the age of the rocks. The oldest fossils (of bacteria) are about 3,500 million years old and are found in rocks formed before the start of the Paleozoic Era. Fossils from this time are rare, probably because the earliest creatures had soft bodies that decayed quickly. By studying fossils, geologists have pieced together the story of life on earth.

LIFE ON EARTH

The story of life on earth began more than 3,500 million years ago. At first, there was no life on earth. The planet was too hot, and its atmosphere too poisonous. Then, gradually, primitive forms of microscopic life evolved in the sea. Over hundreds of millions of years, soft-bodied creatures like jellyfish developed.

Paleozoic Era

At the beginning of this era, there was an explosion of life. Worms, sponges, corals, starfish, graptolites and trilobites all evolved in the warm seas that covered most of the earth during the Cambrian period. Toward the end of the Cambrian, the first fish evolved. More and more new forms of fish and other sea creatures appeared during the Ordovician and Silurian periods and into the Devonian period. During the Devonian, amphibians evolved from fish and began to live on land, but not far from the water in which they still had to lay their eggs. From amphibians evolved reptiles which could live away from water because their eggs had hard shells. During the Permian period, many new reptiles evolved, and some species, including trilobites, became extinct (died out).

Mesozoic Era

More and more reptiles evolved during the Triassic period, including the first dinosaurs. Tiny mammals appeared, too. Ammonites evolved in the sea. During the next period, the Jurassic, the huge sauropod dinosaurs, like Brachiosaurus, evolved. Above their heads flew winged reptiles, called pterosaurs, and the first birds. The Cretaceous saw even more dinosaurs, including the fierce meat-eater, Tyrannosaurus. At the end of the period, and the era, all the dinosaurs died out, along with the ammonites and great sea reptiles.

Cenozoic Era

Now the most important animals were mammals and birds. Horses, elephants, apes and many types of grazing animals appeared during the Tertiary period. During the Quaternary period, human beings appeared.

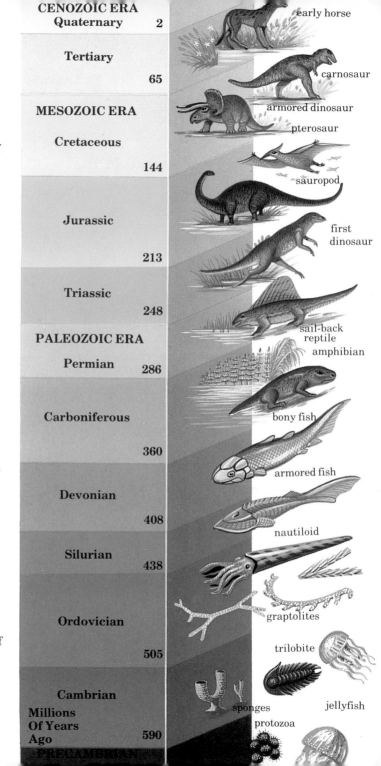

CENOZOIC ERA
Quaternary — 2
Tertiary — 65

MESOZOIC ERA
Cretaceous — 144
Jurassic — 213
Triassic — 248

PALEOZOIC ERA
Permian — 286
Carboniferous — 360
Devonian — 408
Silurian — 438
Ordovician — 505
Cambrian — 590

Millions Of Years Ago

PRECAMBRIAN

early horse
carnosaur
armored dinosaur
pterosaur
sauropod
first dinosaur
sail-back reptile
amphibian
bony fish
armored fish
nautiloid
graptolites
trilobite
jellyfish
sponges
protozoa

geological hammer

trowel

maps, guidebook and compass

fine chisels

dissecting needles

sifter

brushes

helmet and goggles

notebook and pencil

boxes and bags

wrapping paper

labels

Collecting Fossils

Once you know about the rocks you find them in, fossil collecting becomes a more interesting hobby. To start with, it is best to go out with an experienced collector who can tell you what to look for and where and how to recognize your finds.

Fossil remains are nearly always found in sedimentary rocks. You sometimes find them in metamorphic rocks, though usually the shape of the animal's body is twisted beyond recognition by the same forces that changed the surrounding rock. Fossils are not found in igneous rocks. No living tissue could survive the heat of molten rock. The bottom of a cliff is a good place to start looking.

This is the basic equipment you need to start a good fossil collection. When you are collecting, take care of your own safety and respect other people's property. (Ask permission before you collect on private land.) Wear a helmet and goggles when hammering, and don't hammer rocks needlessly. Falling rocks and steep cliffs are dangerous. Never take risks.

When you find a fossil like this ammonite embedded in rock, record where you found it. Then chip it carefully out of the rock. Wrap it carefully and take it home. At home, trim the fossil with fine chisels, identify it if you can, label it and add it to your collection. If you find a fossil mold and cannot remove it, make a plaster cast of it.

Unless you are very lucky, you are unlikely to find the complete skeleton of a Brachiosaurus – though some amateurs have been very successful in the past. Usually, you will find small sea creatures such as trilobites, ammonites and brachiopods. Generally, you will not find a complete petrified fossil. You may not find anything of the animal's body itself. Instead, there may simply be a hollow, or mold, in the rock. If you fill this with plaster of Paris, you can make your own cast.

Pebbles on the Beach

large pebbles

medium-sized pebbles

small pebbles

tiny pebbles

sand

Standing on a beach, you can see the rock cycle in action. The geologist James Hutton (1726-1797) was the first to realize how sedimentary rocks were formed. He watched storm waves breaking against the cliffs, which caused them to crumble. He saw currents of water carrying sand to the sea. He was watching rock in the making. He knew that rivers were also carrying sediment from the land down to the sea. The cycle was endless; there was "no vestige of a beginning, no prospect of an end".

Seashores are either rocky, shingled or sandy. Sand is millions of tiny fragments of rock, pounded almost to dust by the ceaseless churning of the sea.

The pebbles you find on a shingle beach are pieces of cliffs, broken off by waves, or pieces of rock from inland hills and mountains that have been carried to the sea by rivers. The pebbles get their smooth, rounded shapes by being rolled along the riverbed or seabed.

28

On most beaches, the sea has sorted the pebbles neatly into sizes. The biggest are at the top. The tiniest lie on the sand at the edge of the sea. Waves and currents move the pebbles along the shore or out to sea. Even in calm weather, waves keep pebbles on the move. Barriers called groins (far left) are built to keep beaches in place. Pebbles are piled high on one side of the groin and taken away on the other. The action of the sea smooths the pebbles.

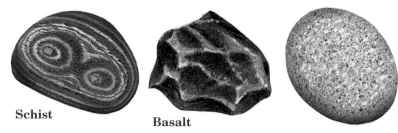

Schist

Basalt

Diabase (dolerite)

Collecting Pebbles

The shape of a pebble is decided mainly by what it is made of. Rocks like granite that have the same hardness all through make oval or ball-shaped pebbles. Slate and shale were laid down in thin layers, so their pebbles are nearly always thin and flat.

If you are lucky, you may find gems or semi-precious stones on the beach, though good quality stones are rare. Most will be forms of quartz or other silicate minerals. You may also find fossils that look like rock. Amber is the fossilized resin of ancient pine trees. Jet is a hard, shiny form of coal.

If you have a rock tumbler, you can polish the stones you collect and make them shiny. If you haven't, they will still look beautiful in a jar of water.

Schists are metamorphic rocks formed originally as layers of mud or silt and later squeezed and baked in the earth's crust. The mud layers show in the pebble in the picture. Diabase is soft enough to be smoothed by the waves. Basalt is found on beaches near volcanoes. Pebbles of the minerals onyx and agate are rare. They are forms of flint with traces of other chemicals which make them beautiful. Jet is a form of very hard coal. Both jet and amber are the relics of ancient trees.

Jet

Agate

Onyx

Amber

Rock Profiles

Names in *italics* have their own entries.

Mudstone

Pumice

Andesite A fine-grained igneous rock formed from volcanoes on land. Named after the Andes Mountains, it is the second most common extrusive igneous rock after *basalt*.

Anthracite See *Coal*.

Arkose A sedimentary rock formed from fragments of granite. It is a type of *sandstone*.

Basalt A fine-grained igneous rock which usually forms from fluid lava on or near the earth's surface. It is the most common extrusive igneous rock formed from lava.

Breccia A sedimentary rock which is made up of sizeable fragments of rock embedded in finer material. It is similar to a *Conglomerate* except that the fragments are sharp and angular rather than rounded.

Chalk See *Limestone*.

Chert See *Flint*.

Coal A sedimentary rock made up of buried plant material. Peat is the first stage of coal formation. Compressed peat is turned into lignite, or brown coal. Further compression turns the lignite into bituminous coal and finally anthracite, which is hard and shiny.

Conglomerate A sedimentary rock made up of rounded pebbles embedded in finer sand or silt. It is sometimes called puddingstone.

Diabase An intrusive igneous rock, also called dolerite.

Diorite An intrusive igneous rock made up of feldspar, hornblende, and other minerals.

Dolerite See *Diabase*.

Dolomite A kind of *limestone* that contains magnesium.

Flint A form of the mineral chalcedony (a kind of silicate), found in lumps in limestone rocks, especially chalk. It sometimes contains fossils. Chert is a variety of flint.

Gabbro A coarse-grained intrusive igneous rock formed from the same kind of magma as *basalt*.

Gneiss The name for a group of metamorphic rocks formed by heat and pressure, often when mountains are being formed.

Granite The most common intrusive igneous rock. It is made of feldspar, quartz and often mica, with smaller amounts of other minerals. Granite is usually mottled and often white, gray, pink or red in color. It appears on the surface when the overlying rocks have been worn away.

Greywacke A kind of *sandstone* containing large sand grains embedded in fine ones.

Hornfels A metamorphic rock formed when heat from magma acts on nearby rocks.

Ignimbrite An igneous rock formed from volcanic ash and volcanic glass. It forms when clouds of hot gas and fine ash erupt from volcanoes.

Kimberlite See *Peridotite*.

Lignite See *Coal*.

Limestone A common sedimentary rock formed mainly from one mineral, calcite. Some limestones are formed mainly from the remains (especially shells) of once-living things. Some are minerals that were once dissolved in water (like stalactites in limestone caves) or oolitic limestones which are

Loess

Chalk

**Basalt
(ropy lava)**

made of masses of rounded grains of calcite. Chalk is one of the purest forms of limestone. It contains the remains of tiny living things called plankton.

Loess A sedimentary rock formed from wind-blown silt or dust.

Marble A metamorphic rock formed when heat and pressure alter *limestone* or *dolomite*. Because it is easy to cut and takes a high polish, it is used to make statues.

Mudstone A sedimentary rock formed from clay that has been compressed.

Obsidian A shiny, glassy extrusive igneous rock used by Stone Age people to make sharp-edged tools.

Peat See *Coal*.

Pegmatite An intrusive igneous rock similar in composition to *granite*, but containing large crystals of minerals, some of which may be rare. Pegmatites are often mined for the minerals they contain.

Peridotite An igneous rock which may have been forced up from the mantle into the crust. A rare kind of peridotite, kimberlite, contains diamonds.

Pitchstone An extrusive igneous rock similar to *obsidian*, but it is dull-looking rather than shiny.

Pumice A light, honeycombed rock formed from frothy lava. It will often float on water.

Quartzite A metamorphic rock formed when heat and pressure change sandstone containing a lot of quartz.

Rhyolite A fine-grained extrusive igneous rock. It often forms plugs in the necks of volcanoes.

Rock salt A rock, mined for salt, which forms when bodies of salty water dry up.

Sandstone A common sedimentary rock formed from grains of sand that have been compressed and cemented together. Sandstones usually form in water, but some red sandstones are the remains of ancient sand dunes.

Schist A group of metamorphic rocks, many of which were formed from *mudstones* and *siltstones*.

Shale A sedimentary rock formed from clay. Unlike *mudstone*, shale is layered and will split into thin sheets.

Siltstone A sedimentary rock formed from particles that are finer than sand, but coarser than clay.

Slate A metamorphic rock formed by heat and pressure on *shale* and sometimes *tuff*. It splits into thin sheets that can be used for roofing houses.

Syenite An intrusive igneous rock similar to *granite*, but much less common. It also contains much less quartz.

Tillite A rock formed from till, which consists of rocky material transported and dumped by glaciers.

Trachyte A fine-grained extrusive igneous rock formed mainly from lava flows.

Tuff A rock formed mainly from volcanic ash.

Index